SLIDING DOWN SUNBEAMS

PRAYERS FOR 4-7 YEAR OLDS

SUSAN HARDWICK

Kevin Mayhew

First published in 1999 by
KEVIN MAYHEW LTD
Buxhall
Stowmarket
Suffolk IP14 3DJ

0 1 2 3 4 5 6 7 8 9

ISBN 1 84003 265 0
Catalogue No. 1500229

Cover design and illustrations by Fred Chevalier
Edited by Elisabeth Bates
Typesetting by Louise Selfe
Printed in Great Britain

Contents

Meet Speck 'n' Fleck

Hi! I'm Speck!

Hiya! And I'm Fleck!

Well, we've been told to write an Intriducshun. (Fleck says I've spelt that wrong.)

We – that's me, Fleck, Zanton and Lamb – hope that you'll like these prayers, and hearing 'bout how we wrote them. We think they're mint.

It's my turn now, Speck.

We've called the prayers *Sliding Down Sunbeams*, 'cos that's what we were doing just before we started writing them.

Speck's just said that prayers are like sunbeams as well, so that could be another reason – that's ever so clever, Speck. Did you just think of that?

Hugs, Fleck. x x
Love, Speck.

Cherubs, Lions and Lambs

Speck slips his arms round the mighty Zanton's neck.

The huge lion lets out his usual roar of pleasure. The sound starts as a low rumble at the back of his throat, and gathers in strength, until it echoes and rings through the clear heavenly air.

Fleck puts her hands over her ears. 'Zanton!' she giggles, 'you're deafenin' me!'

The lion tosses his head, as if to say, 'A lion has to do what a lion has to do.' Then he lowers his massive bulk until his belly is touching the ground.

Speck leaps onto his back, then reaches down a hand to help Fleck up as well. Fleck settles herself comfortably, one leg either side of the lion's muscular back.

Zanton rises to his feet, and begins to pad across the sun-warmed ground, getting quicker and quicker with each step he takes.

'No, Zanton!' protests Speck. 'We haven't got time for a ride now. We've got work to do. . . . We-e-ll, OK then. Just a little, teeny ride.'

Speck sinks his hands into the lion's thick mane, and holds on tight. Fleck holds on tight to Speck.

There could not have been more contrast between the two cherubs – known everywhere in Heaven as Speck 'n' Fleck.

Six-year-old Fleck's long black wavy hair and soft black skin glow in the bright sunlight. Her beautiful, equally dark, dancing eyes have amazing golden flecks – from which she gets her nickname. Fleck finds everything fascinating. And she giggles a lot, because she sees the funny side of nearly everything.

Eight-year-old Speck, on the other hand, has white-blond

hair, and he often frowns as he thinks his deep thoughts.

Now, though, his normally serious sky-blue eyes sparkle with the happiness of being with his beloved Zanton.

Zanton's in a playful mood, and keeps changing direction, suddenly swerving first to the right, then to the left.

Fleck clings on tight to Speck, and Speck clings on tight to the lion's mane, as they gurgle with breathless and excited laughter at Zanton's antics.

Lamb, never far from Zanton's side, follows as best she can, leaping and bleating.

Zanton finally stops on the exact spot they had started from, and sinks down once more onto his belly.

Lamb trots up and settles herself in her favourite place, between his two front legs.

The two cherubs slip off his back, and sit down on either side of Lamb, one on each of the lion's paws.

'You asked Zanton yet? 'bout helping us to write those prayers you and me's got to write?' Fleck says.

Speck shakes his head.

The lion opens one eye slowly and looks at Speck, as if to say, 'Well. Go on then. Ask me.'

Speck shares everything with Zanton. All his secrets. All his problems, and sadnesses and joys. And, when he's finished telling him, he always listens intently to the wise lion's wordless replies.

'Zanton knows everything 'bout everything,' he would say proudly and often. 'I 'spect he's the most wisest lion ever.'

Now, Speck lays his cheek against the great, shaggy mane and whispers into Zanton's ear. Every so often he pauses, and listens intently, a faraway look in those serious, blue eyes.

Fleck, meanwhile, divides her time between watching Speck and Zanton, and cuddling Lamb.

Lamb, in her turn, nuzzles Fleck, bleating softly, her pink tongue gently licking the cherub's face.

'Ooohh, Lamb! That tickles!' giggles Fleck.

Every so often, Fleck stretches out her small wings and flies in circles above the heads of Zanton, Lamb and Speck.

The sun shines down, turning Zanton's coat into gold.

The many coloured leaves of the telinths glow, the light bouncing off them, and sending rainbows into the air.

There the four of them stay – cherubs, lamb and lion, perfectly content to be in each other's company – whilst they write their prayers.

And this is what they wrote:

'Thank You' Prayers

Bags I go first!

'Let's start with some "thank you" prayers,' suggests Fleck, as she flies in circles over the heads of Speck, Zanton and Lamb.

Speck squints up at her, shading his eyes with his hands. The sun is shining down onto her hair, halo and wings, and making her seem like a darting, swirling light as she dances, twists and somersaults.

'Come on down, Fleck. You're making me dizzy,' he laughs.

Fleck does a final circuit, then lands.

'I said, let's start with some "thank you" prayers,' she says again. 'Bags I go first.'

'OK,' agrees Speck.

Fleck chews her pencil thoughtfully for a few minutes, then begins to write . . .

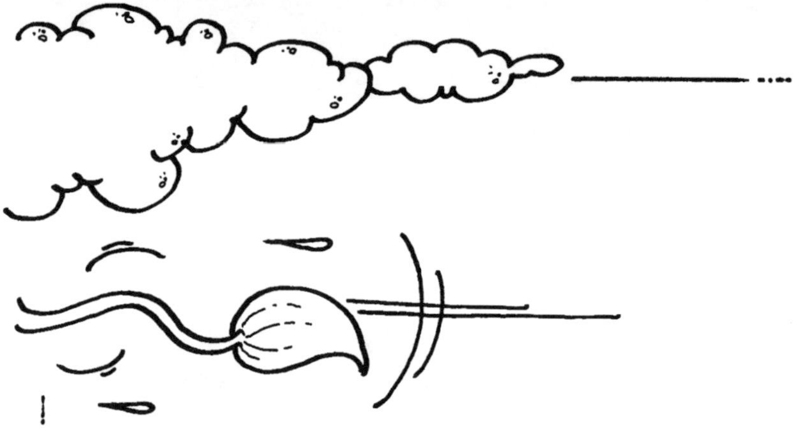

Prayers

Dear Jesus –
I'm bursting with
THANK-U's!

There's so much
I want to share,
that I can't think
which words I want
to say first.
They are all jumbled up
in a heap that's labelled
'Things I want
to thank Jesus for'.

So, Jesus –
thank you
for it all.
Every single bit.

Lots and lots
of love,
Fleck

Thank you,
God,
for my special friends –
for Speck 'n' Fleck.
And Lamb.
And St Francis.

Thank you
for giving me life.

With my biggest,
most grateful roar,
Zanton

Dear God –
THANK YOU
THANK YOU
THANK YOU
thank you, thank you
for EVERYTHING.
I wish I deserved
everything you bless me with.
You really are
very, very
generous and kind,
'cos you pour
your blessings down, anyway,
whether I deserve them
or not.

Speck

Jesus –
thank you for
– grass
– Zanton
– skipping
and running about.

Thank you for
– water
to drink
and to splash in

Thank you for
– my warm, woolly
winter coat.

Your grateful
Lamb.

Dearest Jesus
and God –
thank you for
Mums and Dads
and families.

Thank you for
sky and sun.

Thank you for
friends
and sharing
and playing.

Thank you for
fun and laughter.

Thank you for
school,
and learning,
and brains
to do it with.

Thank you for
birds and animals
('spechally Zanton
and Lamb).

Thank you for
flowers,
and telinths
with their
sparkly,
shining leaves.

Thank you for
all your
love.

All our love,
Fleck 'n' Speck.
x x x x

Prayers for Others

Zanton makes a point

'Now I've said "thank you", can I pray 'bout me?' asks Fleck, hopefully.

A low rumble, starting somewhere deep down inside Zanton, ends in a gentle roar. He shakes his great head and mane slowly from side to side.

The noise fades back once more to a low rumble, then stops.

'Zanton says that, as a rule, we should pray for others before we pray for ourselves,' reports Speck. 'I 'spect he's right.'

Zanton looks at Speck, then at Fleck, with his great, hooded eyes. He nods his head majestically up and down, before resting it back on his huge paws.

'Yep. You're right, Zanton,' agrees Fleck. 'You start this time, Speck . . .'

Prayers

Dear Jesus, God –
please bless
and take care of
all my bestest people.

But, specially,
please will you
help my friend, Tictoc?

He's feeling sad.
Make him happy
once again.

With love from
your grateful friend,
Speck

Jesus –
Zanton's lost his roar.

Please make his throat better.

Sometimes,
when he roars VERY loud,
I wish he wouldn't.

But now he can't,
I miss the sound.

Bleats and bleats of love,
Lamb.

Dear Jesus –
I think there must be
lots and lots
AND LOTS
of people who need you
to take care of them –
just like
you take care of me.

So –
please – will you
look after them as well?

Thank you!
Love and kisses,
Fleck.

God –
people say
I'm a very wise lion.
But I'll never
be as wise
as you.

You
always know
what is best
for each person
and creature
you have made.

So,
I pray that
the right things
will happen
for all your
creation.

Zanton
The-wise-lion-who-
is-not-as-wise-as-
you.

Dear, dearest Jesus –
this is a prayer
for all the lonely,
and sad,
and hurting people
in the
whole wide world.

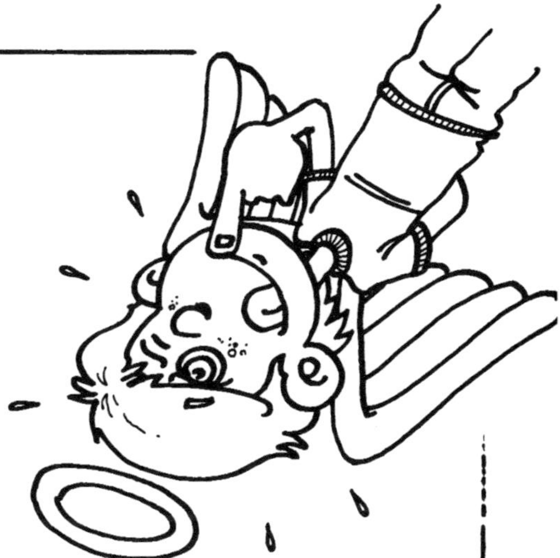

Please
may they know
you are
there for them
always,
and that you are
their very best
friend.

So –
they don't need
to be lonely,
or sad,
or hurting,
any more –
becoz
you are
always
there
FOR
EVERYONE.

Lots and heaps of love,
Speck 'n' Fleck.

Prayers for Me

Tag

'Zanton says now we can pray for us,' says Speck. 'But let's play a game first.'

'Oooh, yes, let's!' agrees Fleck, doing a little twirling dance and ending with a double somersault. 'What shall we play?'

Lamb bumps her head gently against Fleck, then bounds away, before stopping and looking back at the cherubs.

'Lamb wants to play Tag,' laughs Fleck. 'OK, Lamb.' She tags Speck's arm. 'You're "it" now!' She rushes off, with Speck in hot pursuit.

When Speck, Fleck, Lamb and Zanton have each been 'it' several times, they all flop down onto the soft, sun-warmed ground. They are variously gurgling with laughter, bleats and rumbles.

'I love being me,' sighs Speck, lying back and looking up dreamily at the blue, blue sky. 'I wouldn't want to be anyone else. Hey!' He sits up, and grabs a pencil. 'I 'spect that'd make ever such a good prayer . . .'

Prayers

Dear God –
thank you
for making me
me.

I wouldn't
want to be
anyone else.

Being me
is best,
so far as
I'm concerned.

My best love,
Speck. x

Jesus and
God –
how ever so clever
you are
to make us all
so very different.

– All
different shapes,
and colours,
and sizes.

– All
with a
special
part to play
in your world.

– All
with a
special
place
in your heart
and in your love.

Thank you
for making me
the way
I am.

Your special lamb,
Lamb

Jesus –
sometimes
I'm not as nice
and kind
as I should be.

Help me
to be more caring
and loving.

I so want you
to be able
to be proud of me.

All my love,
Fleck.
x o x

God –
you have made me
strong and brave,
and with
a mighty roar.

Help me
to use these,
and all my gifts,
in the service
of others.

May I always give
all glory to you.
Then others will want
to praise your name
and to serve you, too.

Your friend,
Zanton.

Jesus –
you are
EVERYWHERE.

And,
AND
AND
you are
in each one of us.

That's
very
VERY
clever and amazing
to be able
to do both
AT
THE
VERY
SAME
TIME.

We guess
you can do it
becoz you're
God
and
Jesus
rolled into one.

Fleck 'n' Speck.
x o x o x o x

‘I’m Sad’ Prayers

Wideshoes and the ice-flooms

They are just finishing writing the prayers for others, when a voice behind them says, ‘Hiya! It’s me. I’ve just brought you some – oh, yuk! Oh, no! Bother!’

Speck and Fleck look round. They see a young angel, with wild curls and a grubby, dented halo perched over one eye. She is trying to hold three rapidly melting ice-flooms so that they don’t drip all over her.

‘Oooh! Ice-flooms! Thanks, Wideshoes,’ says Fleck excitedly, her eyes lighting up at the sight. ‘What flavours have you got?’

‘Um – aniseed ’n’ chocolate, orange ’n’ marzipan, lime ’n’ fudge,’ said Wideshoes. ‘I mixed them all myself,’ she added proudly.

‘Yuk!’ says Speck.

‘Don’t you want one either, Fleck?’ asks Wideshoes, disappointed. ‘Oh, well. I guess *I’ll* just have to eat them all.’ She plonks herself down on the ground. ‘What are you doing?’

Speck and Fleck read out what they have written so far. Wideshoes listens, and tries at the same time to decide which ice-floom to eat first. As she can’t choose, she takes a lick from each one in turn.

‘They’re ace,’ she says, when Fleck and Speck have finished. ‘Really, reeeelly good.’

‘We’re just about to write some sad, then some happy prayers,’ says Speck.

‘Happy, hap-py, hap-py prayers!’ sings Wideshoes, waving her arms about. The ice-flooms give up the attempt to stay in their containers, fall to the ground, and melt rapidly away.

Wideshoes looks mournfully at the fast-dissolving blobs. 'That'll teach me to be greedy,' she sighs, then jumps to her feet. 'I gotta go. People to see. Things to do. See you! Bye-ee!' She does a couple of cartwheels before skipping off.

As Wideshoes disappears from view, Fleck is busily writing, her tongue between her teeth. 'Listen, Speck,' she says . . .

Prayers

Oh, Jesus! –
I'm really sad.
I don't like
feeling this way.

What is wrong?
Is it me?

Please will you
make me
happy again.

And please,
will you show me
what I must do
as well,
to help you
do this for me.

Love,
Fleck
x x x

Dear Jesus –
the bright sun
has disappeared.

I'm feeling sad.

Please will you
roll away the clouds.
Make the sun
shine again.

Whenever I feel
like this,
please help me
to remember,
all the good things
I have
and that I do,
and all the beautiful
people in my life.

Thank you.
Lamb.

Jesus –
I was not nice
to Fleck.
And now I'm feeling
ever so sad.

I've told her
I'm sorry,
and she said it's OK.

But I still feel bad.
So,
now I'm saying sorry
to you.

If I know you
have forgiven me
as well,
I shall feel better.

Your grateful
Speck.

God –
even lions
as mighty as me
can feel depressed.

But just talking
to you
and telling you
all about it
helps so much.

Now,
help me
to see why
I'm feeling like this.

Then,
help me
to see
what I need
to do to help
make myself feel better.

Your grateful friend,
Zanton.

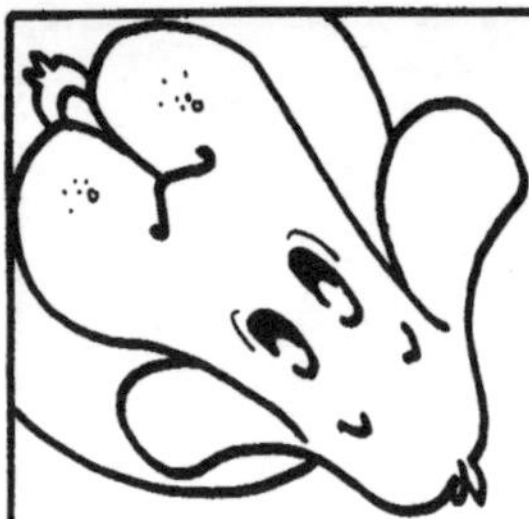

Hey, Jesus! –
you are
always saying
that children
are
extra-special.

Then –
that means
you
extra-specially
care
when
children are sad,
or hurt
in any way.

You kiss away
our tears.
And your
extra-special-children-love
hugs us better.

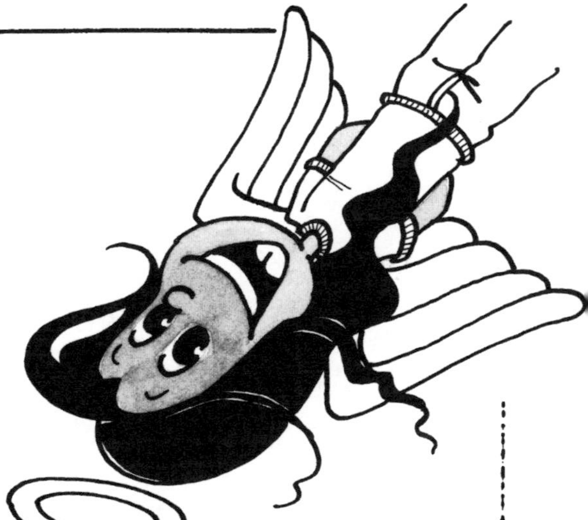

But –
who hugs you better
when you're sad?
Please
can we
do it?
We would really like it
if we could.

Hugs and kisses and love,
Speck 'n' Fleck
x o x o x o x o

'I'm Happy' Prayers

Lamb shares her thoughts

'Well, we've written "thank you" prayers, and prayers for others, and prayers for us,' says Fleck.

'And prayers about being sad,' adds Speck.

'Now we must write some happy prayers. What shall we do after that?' asks Fleck.

They all think for a few moments.

Zanton's great lids droop, as they always do when he's thinking deeply.

Lamb does a few skips and leaps, as it helps her to concentrate.

Fleck's dark eyes, with the amazing golden flecks which sparkle as they catch the sunlight, gaze into the distance.

Speck's blue eyes are serious.

'I know!' he says, suddenly. 'But I'm not going to say until we've done the happy prayers. It's Lamb's turn to start this time.'

Speck kneels in front of Lamb, and slips his arms around her neck. The young angel has no more problem understanding Lamb's bleats than he has understanding Zanton the Lion.

As Lamb shares her thoughts, Speck tells Fleck, and she writes them down.

'Oh, Lamb, that's *bootiful*,' says Fleck . . .

Prayers

Dear God –
my soft voice
is not as loud
as Zanton's
mighty
roar of joy.

But
my heart
is as full
as his.

I'm
so
so
HAPPY!
Thank you!

Thank you
for all the people,
and creatures,
and things,
that make me
feel
like this.

Your own
Lamb.

Wonderful
God!
Most ace
Jesus!
Beautiful
world!

I'm SO happy,
that I want
to dance –
and sing –
and shout –
and laugh
and laugh –
with all that
I feel inside.

I think
I'll burst
if
I don't!

All my love,
Fleck.

Jesus –
I was feeling sad.
Really ever so sad.

But then
I asked you
to make me better.

Now
I feel
like a light's
been switched on
deep inside
of me,
and it's chased
the sadness away.

Thank you
for
happiness!!

Thank you
for showing
your love
in this way.

I love you, too.
Speck.
x x

God –
I'm a very
HAPPY
lion.

I want to make
the heavens shake
with my roar
of joyful
and thankful
praise.

But

happiness is a gift
to pass on
to others,
not just for me
to keep to myself.

And so I pray
you will lead me
to those who need it:

those who are
feeling sad,
for one reason
or another.

Make me a channel
of joy to them.
Zanton.

Jesus and God –
we've bin
counting blessings –
of all the things
that make us
happy.

There were
millions
and trillions
and
zillions
of them!

Thank you
for them all,
every one.

We want
to pray that
all the whole
wide world
will be happy,
and not sad,
any
any
more.

All our love,
Fleck 'n' Speck.

'I Wish' Prayers

All the things we want Jesus and God to help us be and do

'These should be prayers about all the things we want Jesus and God to help us be and do,' says Speck.

Fleck is once again flying in lazy circles above his head, humming softly to herself.

'Fleck! You're making me dizzy again!' he sighs.

'Soz!' she giggles, landing lightly onto Zanton's back, before sliding down his shaggy fur to the ground.

The sun is beginning to slip down in the sky, and the shadows to lengthen.

Fleck is starting to feel sleepy. She yawns, then sits down next to Speck. They both lean against Zanton's side, as they think about what they want to write . . .

Jesus –
you are always saying
we should
ask you for
everything
we want
or need.

So –
I want to ask
that all
girls and boys,
EVERYWHERE,

will know you
and your love,
just like
Speck
and me do.

Please
make this wish
come true!

I love you!
Fleck.
x x x

Jesus and God –
my wish is
that
Speck 'n' Fleck
will grow
in their love
of you,
every single day.

And
that they
will become
more and more
and more like you
as they grow
in body,
and mind,
and soul,
and spirit.

Zanton.

God –
I wish –
I wish –
I wish for so
many things,
that I don't know
what to
ask for first.

I 'spect
I'll just have to
wrap them all
into a bundle
and give them
to you.

Then,
you can choose
which ones
are right
and best
for me.

Thanks for being
so wise
and understanding
of all my needs.
Speck.
x o x

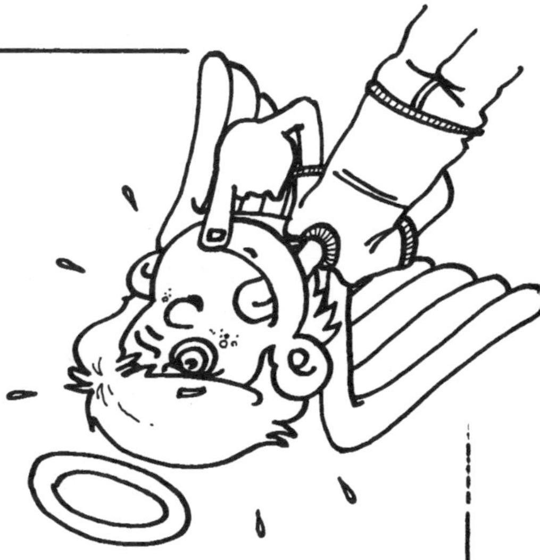

Jesus –
I wish
that your love
will spill out
to fill
everyone's
hearts,
and the
whole world.

Then,
Heaven
will live on
earth
and fill it
all over.

Then,
there will be
no place
where you are not.

Love,
Lamb.

Jesus –
we made
a thank you list.
Now,
we've made a
wish list.

It's full of things
we want you
to help us
be and do.

So – here it is.

Help us always
to be kind
and not selfish.

Help us always
to think of others
and not just
ourselves.

Help us always
to be thankful
for all the
good things
in our lives.

Help us always
to be loving
and caring.

Help us always
to grow
every single day
more
and more
like
YOU.

All our love,
Speck 'n' Fleck.
xxx ooo xxx

Amen

Zanton yawns, his mighty mouth opening wide.

He tries to stretch his legs without disturbing the sleeping cherubs, who are curled up against his great, shaggy mane.

Both Fleck and Speck are dreaming the same dream. They are dreaming that they are sliding down glowing, sparkling, golden sunbeams. At the end of one of the sunbeams, Wideshoes is standing, holding lots and lots of ice-flooms.

'I mixed them all myself,' she is saying proudly.

In between them, Lamb also sleeps, dreaming of leaping and playing on soft green grass.

The sun is sinking down, and a rainbow of colours is splashed across the sky, making it look like a child's painting, so beautiful are the colours.

The completed prayers lie on the ground nearby.

Zanton's eyes start to close contentedly.

It is the end of another heavenly day.